REAL-WORLD PROJECTS TO EXPLORE WORLD WAR II

rosen publishing's
rosen central®
New York

ANGIE TIMMONS

Published in 2019 by The Rosen Publishing Group, Inc.
29 East 21st Street, New York, NY 10010

First Edition

Library of Congress Cataloging-in-Publication Data

Names: Timmons, Angie, author.
Title: Real-world projects to explore World War II / Angie Timmons.
Description: New York : Rosen Central, 2019. | Series: Project-based learning in Social Studies | Includes bibliographical references and index. | Audience: Grades: 5–8.
Identifiers: LCCN 2017056516| ISBN 9781508182283 (library bound) | ISBN 9781508182290 (pbk.)
Subjects: LCSH: World War, 1939–1945—Juvenile literature.
Classification: LCC D743.7 .T56 2018 | DDC 940.53—dc23
LC record available at https://lccn.loc.gov/2017056516

Manufactured in the United States of America

CONTENTS

World War II is arguably one of the most significant events in history. The conflict redefined warfare and introduced a form of weaponry that catapulted the world into secretive hostilities that still plague international relations. From the beginning of the war, with the late 1930s Japanese and German invasions of their neighboring countries, to the utter devastation that brought about the end of the war in 1945, the war's tentacles touched nearly every part of the globe. The trench warfare of World War I—the war that was supposed to "end all wars"—was gone. World War II took the fighting to the air, the sea, and even hidden spaces. World War II gave rise to the industrialism and innovation that produced sophisticated, powerful weapons and the evolution of wartime code and code-breaking technologies.

The United States and its allies fought a war on two fronts: Europe and the Pacific. Combatants on both sides used new technologies and techniques that could wipe out thousands of people with one air raid. One submarine warhead could cripple

In August 1942, Allied troops landed on the Solomon Islands for the Battle of Guadalcanal. The fighting lasted six months and ended with a major Allied victory in the Pacific.

another nation's naval force or destroy its supply of food and other resources.

There was little distinction between civilians and the military in World War II. As fanatical powers rose, invaded, and carried out horrific atrocities against innocent people, everyone and everything became a target. Such atrocities both began and ended the war.

Project-based learning, or PBL, is a great way to learn the nuances of a complex conflict that launched the United States to become the world's foremost global superpower, introduced the military-industrial complex, changed the face of global boundaries, and spawned generations of further conflict.

In a conflict as complicated, fascinating, and emotional as World War II, traditional methods of teaching, such as lectures and the study of thick textbooks, are rife with the potential for important details to fall through the cracks. PBL puts students in charge of how they learn. Using PBL, students engage with subject matter over an extended period through investigation, dynamic group collaboration, decision-making, problem-solving, reflection, and public presentation. PBL asks students to frame subject matter within a real-world context by tying areas of study to current events and personal concerns.

While World War II is a fascinating chapter in history, its complicated web can make it a difficult study. PBL removes much of that difficulty and adds in an interdisciplinary approach that puts students in the driver's seat.

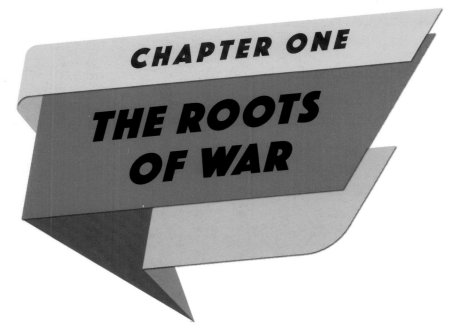

CHAPTER ONE

THE ROOTS OF WAR

Many historians now view the Japanese invasion of China in 1937—also considered the beginning of the Second Sino-Japanese War—as the start of World War II. Largely obscured by the global battles that raged over the next eight years, the Sino-Japanese conflict was a harbinger of what was to come in World War II: fanatical viewpoints, violent invasions motivated by ideas of racial superiority and expansionism, the use of superior industrial and military might against less-equipped nations, and horrific atrocities toward military personnel and civilians alike.

In the Japanese invasion and occupation of the Chinese city of Nanjing, now commonly referred to as the Rape of Nanjing, tens of thousands of women were raped and murdered. Survivors and witnesses tell of babies and small children speared with bayonets, prisoners of war buried and burned alive, civilians and prisoners of war shot in the back, and a Yangtze River that ran red with blood for days on end. Nanjing was an early example of the hate-fueled genocide and war crimes for which World War II has become known.

At the same time, an obscure radical movement had risen to power in Germany and was poised to bring Europe to its knees. Adolf Hitler and the Nazi Party led a campaign to eliminate and exterminate non-Aryans and create a world for his Germanic master race. On his march toward global domination, Hitler gathered strange bedfellows to his cause and aggressively began seizing territories.

In 1933, seven years before the outbreak of global hostilities in World War II, Adolf Hitler rallied the German people to support the dictator's vision for a racially pure Germany.

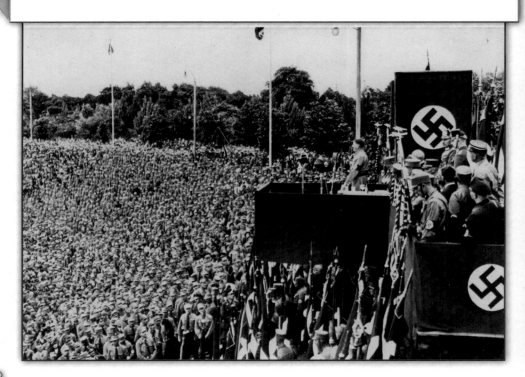

By 1940, Japan and Germany had sealed an alliance fueled by expansionist desires and notions of racial superiority. Italian dictator Benito Mussolini, who had allied with Hitler in 1936, joined the war in 1940 by declaring war on a historic rival: France. The alliance of Germany, Japan, and Italy, commonly called the "Axis powers" or "Axis," would become the focus of

ITALY'S ROLE

Following Allied successes in the Balkans and North Africa, Mussolini was ousted by senior Italian military officials and politicians in the summer of 1943. Germany acted swiftly. A group of German special forces rescued Mussolini from a detention center in the Abruzzi mountains, placed him at the lead of a puppet state in Northern Italy, and rapidly disarmed every Italian soldier they could find. Germany continued to occupy Italy despite its surrender to the Allies, spurring Italian and German unrest. The Allied forces were able to turn much of Italy toward an anti-Axis sentiment, which helped the Allied forces as they made a bloody march north through the Italian peninsula. In 1945, an Italian resistance group captured and publicly executed Mussolini.

Despite its brief and often ambiguous role in World War II, Italy caused Allied forces to devote troops in the Mediterranean, North Africa, and Italy itself while war raged elsewhere. Though the nation eventually turned toward the Allied cause, the recruitment effort was bloody and long.

a conflict that spread far beyond Japan's attacks on mainland Asia and Hitler's commencing march across Europe. Arrayed against the Axis powers were the Allied powers, or Allies. Key allied nations included Britain, China, the Soviet Union, and the United States, though the latter two did not join the Allies until 1941.

QUESTION: HOW DID JUST TWO NATIONS BRING THE WORLD TO WAR?

In the Far East, Japan had been an isolated nation since the seventeenth century. This long history of isolation preserved its culture and what the Japanese regarded as their racial superiority. In the mid-nineteenth century, American warships entered Tokyo Bay, and American officials strong-armed the shocked and terrified Japanese into agreeing to port, shipping, and trade agreements that would enhance America's trade routes into mainland Asia. Seeing that Japan's isolationism had caused it to fall behind the rest of the world in military technologies, the country's government adopted and enforced a strict moral code for all citizens (*bushidō*, the samurai code of "the way of the warrior") and rapidly industrialized. Fervent nationalist and expansionist theories grew. To grow its industry and military, Japan needed natural resources, which it could only get through trade with nations like the United States and its neighbors in mainland Asia. This need, coupled with strong national ideals of racial superiority, sent Japanese troops abroad in a bloody march across Asia and a devastating flight across the Pacific Ocean.

As punishment for Germany's aggression in World War I, the United States, Britain, and France instituted the demands of the Treaty of Versailles: war reparations, loss of land, and a substantial decrease in the German military. A decade later, Germany and the rest of the world were suffering from the Great Depression of the 1930s. Unemployed and desperate Germans, many of whom were already angry at the harsh terms of the Treaty of Versailles, blamed their parliamentary government for being weak.

A powerful and emphatic speaker driven by a seemingly endless supply of fervor, Hitler promised prosperity, the reversal

Japanese soldiers march in a celebratory parade in 1936, before departing for Japanese-controlled Manchuria.

of the Treaty of Versailles, and the restoration of German culture if his Nazi Party was elected. The Nazis launched a massive propaganda campaign that directed the Germans' impatience, anger, and fear toward specific groups, such as the Jews. By the mid-1930s, the Nazis came to power, and the party's Führer, Hitler, propagated ideas of Germanic racial superiority and the threat that other races and ethnic groups posed to the Germans.

PROJECT
IMPERIAL ENDEAVORS AND RACIAL SUPERIORITY

The theater of war is the area in which the fighting in a war takes place. World War II had two theaters of war: the European theater and the Pacific theater. Mapping out some of the key events of the war can make it easier to grasp just why it was called a "world war."

- *Research the movements of Axis forces beginning in the 1930s and into the early years of World War II. Learn about the motivations and goals behind each invasion. Consider factors such as imperial desires, the quest for natural resources, ideas of racial or ethnic superiority, and a history of friction between nations (for example, Japan and China or Germany and France).*

- *Start making a virtual map of the globe with mobile graphics (such as arrows, moving ships, and flying airplanes). Helpful tools for this project include ZeeMaps and Mapline. The History Channel's WWII from Space documentary provides a good example of how a virtual globe, virtual mapping techniques, and the use of graphics work.*

- *Pick two examples of invasions by Axis powers—one in the Pacific theater and one more in the European theater—that had a* big impact on how the early years of the war unfolded. Use mobile graphics to show each of these invasions. You can use a different color to represent each country's forces.

- Drawing on what you learned in your research, add explanations of the motivation behind each invasion to the map. The written explanation should be a brief note, overlaying each graphic.
- Research current examples of nationalist, racist, and cultural conflicts that have led to aggression. Consider areas like Russia, Ukraine, Syria, and other parts of the Middle East. Add one of these to your map, including a written explanation.
- Present your virtual map to your class. Lead a discussion about both the current-day and World War II-era events illustrated on your map.

QUESTION: WHAT ROLE DID GEOGRAPHY PLAY IN THE RISE AND CONFLICT OF WORLD WAR II, AND WHAT ROLE HAS WORLD WAR II PLAYED IN MODERN-DAY GEOGRAPHY AND CONFLICTS?

Starting close to home, Hitler moved his army rapidly against Germany's neighbors and traditional enemies. In 1939, Hitler made a secret pact with Soviet leader Joseph Stalin for a joint invasion of Poland. Germany invaded western Poland, while the Soviets invaded eastern Poland. The world, including the

The Luftwaffe, the aerial warfare branch of the German military, used fire bombs to devastate the Polish city of Warsaw shortly after Hitler's invasion in 1939.

United States, watched what happened in Poland, but only a few nations mobilized against Hitler.

Aggressions in Asia had already been underway for, in some cases, decades. Japan made several military forays into Russia and mainland Asia beginning in the 1880s. By 1941, Japan held large areas of China and had turned its sights on Southeast Asia, invading Indochina in July 1941. This invasion prompted US president Franklin D. Roosevelt to freeze Japanese assets in America, effectively cutting off trade with Japan.

In the early twentieth century, Americans held dear the idea of noninvolvement in global affairs. America had entered World War I, but was late in doing so. The 1920s and the Great Depression of the 1930s only made Americans more isolationist. Buffered on both sides by enormous oceans, Americans felt protected and wanted to focus on their own economic recovery rather than become involved in the affairs of distant nations. Japan's attack on Pearl Harbor, Hawaii, on December 7, 1941, showed Americans that their ocean buffers did not make them impervious to attack.

PROJECT
THE LEGACY OF BATTLE AND SELF-PRESERVATION

The United States joined the Allies against the Axis late in 1941. As the war raged and the need to secure vital resources and protect those resources' lines of transportation became wars in themselves, geography was forever impacted by more than just battles.

The list below includes important incidents, events, operations, and actions relating to World War II. For instance, interference in developing nations in the Middle East and Africa during that period is responsible for many of today's hostilities. Use this list to begin research and find other examples of events from World War II that had long-lasting effects. Then write an essay focusing on the impacts of one of these events on the map of the world today.

- The Treaty of Versailles and a disintegrating Germany
- The Japanese invasion of China and other mainland Asian nations
- The Japanese invasion of Indochina
  - *Consider the French aspect of this aggression and how it affected the Allies*
- The invasion of Poland in 1939
- The Soviet invasions and aggressions in Baltic nations (for example, Finland)
- The German invasions in Europe between April and June 1940
- Operation Dunkirk
- Italy's entrance into the war
  - *Consider the impact of Italy's involvement on the Mediterranean and North Africa*
- The Pearl Harbor attack
- The German invasion of the Soviet Union and how a winter won a battle
- The Battle of Britain
- The Anglo-Iraqi War and Farhud
- The Syria-Lebanon Campaign
- The Anglo-Soviet Invasion of Iran
- Operation Torch
- Operation Compass

QUESTION: HOW DID ECONOMIC SANCTIONS, SUCH AS EMBARGOES, PROMPT ACTIONS LEADING UP TO AND DURING WORLD WAR II?

In the late 1930s and early 1940s, American trade embargoes against Japan limited Japan's access to oil. Japan retaliated with the bombing of Pearl Harbor, which caused America to enter the war.

These actions only scratch the surface of the various trade embargoes and limitations to trade that led to hostilities. Germany was the subject of restricted trade in the years leading up to the war, which caused resentment among its citizens and power brokers. Germans were led by charismatic leaders like Hitler in the blaming of ethnic groups they accused of hoarding resources and disrupting German racial superiority.

PROJECT
THE INSTABILITY THAT CAUSED WAR

Study and track the various trade-related actions that caused economic instability and downturn among World War II's main aggressors, Germany and Japan. Investigate how trade relations compelled to Italy enter an alliance with the other Axis powers.

- *Economic factors encompass many cause-effect relationships that go beyond money; research how Japanese and German racial superiority fed and empowered those nations' pursuit of resources—resources they believed they had an inherent right to possess.*
- *Using design software, create colorful, easy-to-read cause-and-effect match cards to*

In project-based learning, students lead the discussions, either as part of their group presentation, or to follow a presentation and learn what their classmates think about the topic.

help classmates understand the specific economic causes that affected World War II. Make the details specific enough that classmates can identify which nation felt the cause, but general enough that peers can identify the nation involved and apply critical thinking to determine effect (for example: "War reparations from past aggressions/ conflicts" would be a cause card, and

"Germans felt resentment among its population" would be an effect).

- *Helpful tools for this project include cause-and-effect diagramming tools, such as SmartDraw, Microsoft Excel or Visio, Apple Sheets, and Lucidchart. For printable cause-and-effect cards, programs such as Microsoft Word can serve as a starting point. Images can be found through tools, such as Freepik and Pixabay, and text and photo editors, such as Typorama and Piktochart, can help in the design process.*

- **Present the cause-and-effect match cards to your class. Following the presentation, discuss how current embargoes, sanctions, and strained trade relations that impact political and economic relations between nations today (for example, the United States and North Korea, and the Iran nuclear deal).**

CHAPTER TWO

THE WAR EFFORT

When the United States joined the war in late 1941, it did so on the heels of the greatest economic depression the world had ever experienced. While Germany and Japan had spent the last decade compelling their populations to put nation before self and rapidly industrializing, the United States had limped out of the Great Depression by pouring massive federal resources into the New Deal, President Roosevelt's sweeping economic reform effort that put Americans back to work.

Britain and other European nations were already war weary and recovering from the global economic downturn of the 1930s. China, Japan's biggest target, was amid a prolonged civil war between rival governing factions.

Following Hitler's six-month-long invasion of the Soviet Union in 1940, the Soviets were destitute. Hitler's scorched-earth invasion left villages, cities, countryside, and crops burned to the ground. Tens of millions of Soviets had died as Hitler chased the Red Army toward Moscow. The Soviets turned to the Allies for help, effectively joining against the Axis, but with little more than a small cache of depleted resources. For the Allied powers to slow down the Axis, major changes would have to happen.

QUESTION: HOW DID CIVILIANS CONTRIBUTE TO THE WAR EFFORT, AND HOW DID THE COMMON GOOD AND PROTECTION/GROWTH OF RIGHTS PROMPT THEIR CONTRIBUTIONS? HOW DID CIVILIAN INVOLVEMENT FOREVER CHANGE THE FACE OF SOCIETY?

Just a few years earlier, Americans had largely backed isolationist policies, wanting no part in the wars of foreign nations. However, wartime realities rallied the American people like never before. Propaganda, food and goods rations, and higher taxes served as daily reminders that American armed forces needed the sacrifices and contributions of the American people.

Like their Axis counterparts, Allied nations used radio, newspaper, and magazine ads to rally their people into supporting the war. These advertisements were heavy on images and messaging that stirred fear and patriotism. This kind of public outreach is called propaganda. It rallied public support to the cause by suggesting Americans' freedom was at risk. Before December 1941, Americans had little fear of foreign invasion. The Pearl Harbor attack changed that. The American government capitalized on that newfound vulnerability by doubling taxes to help fund the war, but also by selling war bonds.

Though the bonds offered a rate of return below market value, they represented a moral, financial, and patriotic stake

Propaganda like this poster, which encouraged Americans to grow victory gardens, generated widespread support for the war. Civilians did all they could on the homefront in World War II.

in the war. To sell bonds, celebrities like Bette Davis and Rita Hayworth embarked on a "Stars Over America" bond blitz, during which they visited more than 300 cities and towns to promote the purchase of war bonds. On Civilian D-Day in 1944, planes flying over Chicago dropped thousands of ads asking citizens to buy war bonds. The Girls Scouts helped by donating one stamp each (worth ten cents) and trading them in to purchase of war bonds.

Movie theaters held free movie days—well, admission was granted with a war bond purchase. A sixteen-hour CBS

PROGRESS ON THE HOMEFRONT

With nearly every able-bodied male between the ages of eighteen and forty-five sent to fight, civilian employment in the United States rose from forty-six million in 1940 to more than fifty-three million in 1945. Women and African Americans, still subject to segregation in the armed forces, made substantial gains in employment in America during the war.

Executive Order 8802 prohibited racial discrimination in job training programs and by defense contractors and established a Fair Employment Practices Committee to ensure compliance. By the end of 1944, nearly two million black people were at work in defense industries. Women entered the workforce in huge numbers, symbolized by the Rosie the Riveter campaign. Income levels rose for nearly all workers.

radio broadcast netted nearly forty million dollars in war bonds. The New York Yankees, Brooklyn Dodgers, and New York Giants allowed admission to certain games with the purchase of a war bond. These athletic events generated $56.5 million in war bond sales. By the end of World War II, more than eighty-five million Americans had purchased $185.7 billion in war bonds.

For Americans, the military was not the only segment of society fighting the war. Average, everyday citizens saw their contributions (taxes, food, entry into the workforce) and their sacrifices (such as rations) as their way of fighting oppressive regimes such as Japan and Germany. Everyday Americans rallied under the banner of freedom, giving up crops, financial resources, time, and other resources for the good of the war effort.

PROJECT
FIGHTING THE WAR FROM HOME

Explore how examples of propaganda encouraged civilian action in World War II and how it ended up changing American society even after the war.

- *Find at least fifteen different examples of American propaganda from World War II. Image research tools include Google Images, Google Scholar, and the Library of Congress's Prints & Photographs Online Catalog.*
  - *Look for examples of the ubiquitous Rosie the Riveter poster that encouraged women to*

enter the workforce by empowering women to think of themselves as soldiers on the home front. Rather than the typical feminine stereotypes used to appeal to women in pre–World War II generations, Rosie the Riveter presented a stronger female ideal.

- *Also look for posters celebrating the entry of black Americans into the skilled labor force and the military. One group to look for*

A young man listens to an audio guide while viewing a World War II-era war bonds poster at the Kenosha History Center in Wisconsin. War bonds funded much of America's World War II involvement.

is the Tuskegee Airmen. An all-black unit, the Tuskegee Airmen (also called the Red Tails for their planes' distinctive red markings), flew more than 15,000 bomber escorts. The first African American aviators in a United States still governed by Jim Crow laws, the Red Tails were part of a still-segregated military. However, the unit grew in its distinction and developed a reputation for successful escorts. Originally shunned by the white military, the Red Tails eventually acquired the right to fly combat missions. Three years after World War II ended, the American military finally desegregated. In an increasingly industrialized America, black laborers found opportunities in skilled labor that supported innovation and militarization.

- Compile these images into a slideshow, and before each image, insert an introductory slide that explains the image's significance to the wartime effort.
- Conclude the slideshow with slides exploring the lasting impact of civilian involvement in the war effort. Use a few slides to summarize your thoughts on what motivated civilians of all types to sacrifice and move away from traditional roles. In your summary, point out the emotional and patriotic motivations that guided American civilians. To explore the lasting impact, consider how World War II

moved women away from typical domesticity and into skilled labor. Consider how the war moved black people and other minorities into more skilled professions. Summarize how those groups ultimately benefited from their involvement in World War II, and how you believe this civic involvement changed the United States forever (for instance, workplace integration and two-income households).

QUESTION: WHAT ROLE DID SPEECHES BY LEADERS PLAY IN INSPIRING THE PEOPLE OF EACH NATION TO FIGHT?

In many of Adolf Hitler's speeches, the tyrant emphatically shouted ideas of racial superiority to cheering crowds. Today, his words make most of us shudder. However, in the era of World War II, Hitler's words and the way he delivered them helped send the world into chaos.

While the speeches of Hitler and his Axis ally, the Italian dictator Benito Mussolini, were

Italian dictator Benito Mussolini joined Hitler in forming the Axis powers.

impassioned, emphatic, full of gestures, and used powerful, emotive language, the Allied powers had their share of memorable speeches. President Franklin D. Roosevelt made several profound speeches, as did famous orator and British Prime Minister Winston Churchill. Roosevelt and Churchill spoke largely about an end to the war or the lengths they would go to end hostilities. Hitler and Mussolini had very different messages.

PROJECT
STIRRING SPEECHES

Allied leaders, such as US president Franklin D. Roosevelt and British prime minister Winston Churchill, are still remembered for their eloquent and inspiring speeches.

- *Find several speeches delivered by Churchill and Roosevelt during World War II. Speeches can be found through Internet research, on YouTube, and through digital archives such as those offered by the Library of Congress and the British Broadcasting Corporation (BBC).*
- *What tools do Churchill and Roosevelt use to make their points?*
  - *Take note of the tone of the speeches.*
  - *Write down turns of phrase that are especially inspiring.*
- *Compile images of these leaders delivering speeches and snippets of some of the most impactful statements from notable speeches.*

- *Create a blog or presentation that includes the images, speeches, and statements found in the research. Detail the differences in how the leaders addressed their publics. Possible blogging tools include WordPress and Google Sites. Presentation tools include Google Slides, PowerPoint, and Prezi.*
  - *Discuss the effect the speeches' words and overall delivery affected World War II-era society and the impact studying those speeches had on the group during research and project creation.*
  - *Share a conclusion about how these leaders could rally entire nations to make life-changing choices and actions with the power of their words.*

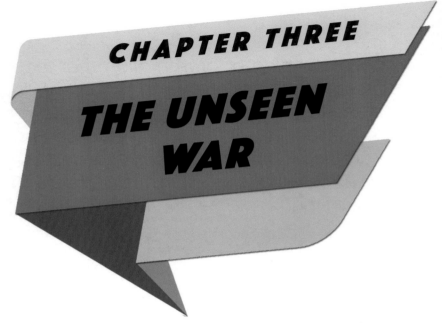

CHAPTER THREE

THE UNSEEN WAR

In the modern age of constant communication and news on demand, imagining a world in which the global population is unaware of major atrocities or war crimes is almost unthinkable. When witnesses to crimes or acts of hate can simply record video or audio using their smartphones and immediately upload the file to social media, today's actions are shared instantaneously.

The atmosphere of mistrust and the race to outdo the enemy's military capabilities kept many World War II–era innovations and technologies top secret. Secret codes were developed, the early precursors to stealth technologies were adopted on warships and aircraft carriers, and missions were planned and implemented for months before they were carried out.

Unfortunately, even darker secrets were kept hidden in World War II. Concentration camps, the full extent of Japanese brutality in China and Asia's mainland, and the American internment of Japanese Americans during the war are conspicuously missing from World War II headlines. The hostilities and covert actions that often steered the war out of plain sight have ended up as some of World War II's most horrifying tales.

After Germany's surrender to the Allied forces in 1945, Allied soldiers forced many German citizens to visit concentration camps, which were sometimes just a couple of miles away from German homes and villages. These camps, where millions of Jews were starved, gassed, and burned to death throughout the German Holocaust, were a surprise to many average German citizens. Footage of their forced visits to the concentration camps shows some Germans collapsing in shock and anguish, while others became ill at the sight of piles of dead bodies and wraithlike camp survivors.

A HORROR LIKE NO OTHER

While the mass graves and piles of skeletal corpses were beyond horrifying in their own right, they did not expose the concentration camps' other morbid secrets. Human experiments were performed on Jewish concentration camp prisoners, including children and adults alike. Some of the secret details of the camps' sordid medical and scientific were spirited away by Nazi loyalists before the Allies descended upon them. Some Nazi and SS officials were hunted down across Europe, South America, and other parts of the globe in the decades to follow and brought to justice by international courts. Others were never found.

QUESTION: WHAT CAN WE LEARN FROM THE VICTIMS AND SURVIVORS OF THE HOLOCAUST AND THE RAPE OF NANJING?

Among the books read in schools, few are as haunting or profound as those about the Holocaust, such as Elie Wiesel's *Night* or *The Diary of Anne Frank*. Wiesel was orphaned and imprisoned during the Holocaust. Anne Frank was a young German-born Jewish girl who kept a diary while her family was in hiding in the Netherlands, attempting to evade capture by the Gestapo (a Nazi-run police force charged with finding

Though Anne Frank died in a concentration camp, the diary she kept while in hiding has endured as an emotional reminder of the horror of the Holocaust.

and gathering Jews to send them to concentration camps). The Gestapo found her family in 1944, sent them to the camps, and Anne died within a few months. Her diary has become an icon in the study of Nazi persecution of the Jewish people.

Many Holocaust survivors have testified, and their stories have been recorded for museums and other Holocaust memorial efforts. The Allied forces that liberated the camps also gathered evidence of the camps' horrors. Many Allied soldiers admit they became emotionally and physically ill at what they witnessed upon entering the camps. Images of gas chambers, ovens in which the Nazis burned prisoners alive, and piles of skeletal corpses were soon circulated for worldwide consumption. Those prisoners found alive were usually barely hanging on to life, and typically had lost most of their family and friends to the Nazis.

Farther east, the oft-overlooked Rape of Nanjing was an atrocity in its own right. When Japan invaded China and advanced up the Yangtze River, the Imperial Army conquered the historic and walled city of Nanjing. During the first couple months of Japan's occupation of the city, Japanese soldiers waged a war of terror against Chinese civilians and the few Chinese soldiers who'd survived the battles up the Yangtze. Thousands died. Women and young girls were raped by the tens of thousands. The elderly, children, and babies were murdered, and hundreds died of starvation and illness. Though some of those who survived did so due to the intervention of westerners living in the city at the time of the Japanese invasion, the world largely failed to intervene on Nanjing's behalf. Even after Japanese bombers sank a US ship in the Yangtze right outside of Nanjing, the United States did not come to the city's aid.

Documentaries, books, and stories about the victims of the European Holocaust abound. While the Nanjing massacre has not been as well documented, more records and witness testimonies from both the Chinese and Japanese perspective have been unearthed in the last couple of decades.

PROJECT
AN ORAL HISTORY

Today many of us live lives that are more peaceful than anything people from the World War II era could have imagined. This makes bearing witness and passing on the stories of the war's victims critical. Not only do we need to thoroughly understand the trials and horrors endured by World War II's genocide victims, but we also need to identify conditions in our modern world that hint at the potential for racial, ethnic, or cultural persecution.

- *Break up into teams of two to four students to research personal accounts of victims of the Holocaust, the Rape of Nanjing, and other persecutions carried out during World War II.*

  - *If you know of any survivors of the Holocaust or the Rape of Nanjing, ask them if they would be willing to discuss the events with you. Guidance on conducting oral histories can be found in the Oral History Association's "Web Guides to Doing Oral History" and at DoHistory.org.*

Some Holocaust survivors have shared their tragic stories with the public. Will Satloff (*left*) thanked Holocaust survivor Nesse Godin for telling her story at his school in Silver Spring, Maryland, in 2012.

- *Also look for firsthand accounts that others have recorded. The histories may come from survivors or be records of people who died at the hands of their persecutors.*
- Pick out the most compelling stories for a presentation to your class. Have each member of the group tell one person's story while a slideshow of related images plays behind the group's orators.
  - *Slideshow tools include Microsoft PowerPoint, Prezi, PresentationTube, Pathbrite, and Apple Keynote.*

QUESTION: WHAT ASPECTS OF WORLD WAR II TOOK PLACE BEHIND THE SCENES?

Behind the serene White Cliffs of Dover on England's southeastern tip—just 20 miles (32 kilometers) from French shores, across the English Channel—is a labyrinthine system of tunnels that hosted some of Britain's most significant World War II operations and secrets.

An entryway to these tunnels sits tucked under Dover Castle, which has stood sentry over England's most vulnerable shoreline since the eleventh century. Modern visitors can penetrate deeper into the cliff through these tunnels, visiting rooms where Churchill and other powerful Allied leaders planned, strategized, and green-lit now-famous World War II actions. From Dover, Britain launched the rescue mission at Dunkirk. This nine-day mission saw British civilian and military vessels alike cross the perilous British Channel, under fire from German bombers, to rescue 339,000 soldiers trapped by German artillery on a northern French beach. The tunnels were home to messengers who sent British code far and wide, as well as home to operations that sent false messages to mislead the Axis powers. When the Cold War broke out in the late 1940s, the tunnels were repurposed as a refuge that could survive nuclear attacks.

The Dover tunnels are just one example of the part of World War II that was waged unseen. London was filled with similar subterranean spots that kept leaders safe from constant German bombing so that Allied actions and missions could still be approved and carried out. Hitler himself was fond of underground bunkers. In fact, he met his end in one in Berlin.

Due to their proximity to mainland Europe, the tunnels carved behind the White Cliffs of Dover in England were home to several major Allied efforts, including intelligence gathering through cables.

PROJECT
EXPLORING UNDERGROUND

Much of World War II happened out in the open— pitched battles on land, at sea, and through air raids and bombs. However, many powerful decisions were made in World War II's hidden centers of power, such as underground bunkers and the maze of tunnels in Dover. These out-of-sight spaces were the launchpads of some of the war's most high-profile operations.

- *Divide up into teams of two or three students. Research one of the hidden locations that proved important in the war.*
- *Take the class through a virtual tour of underground bunkers in Berlin, London, Dover, and other hidden or obscured sites used by World War II leaders.*
  - *The team can use existing virtual tours or tourists' videos of such spaces to guide its own virtual tour. Virtual tour programs include Animoto, WondaVR, and LiveTour.*
  - *Ensure your virtual tour allows viewers to see the full scope of how these underground areas were accessed, how they were often hidden in plain sight, how extensive they were, and which rooms within these subterranean power centers served which purposes, as well as who used them—and who died in them.*

QUESTION: WHAT ROLE DID CRYPTOGRAPHY PLAY IN WORLD WAR II?

The Enigma machine (also called Victory) was essentially a typewriter that encrypted secret messages. British code breakers, housed at an English Victorian manor called Bletchley Park, used it to decipher German traffic signals during World War II. The machine was German-created. The intelligence shared by the Enigma machine was called Ultra. Very few British officials knew its inner workings or even of its existence.

The center of British intelligence in World War II, Bletchley Park is where cryptographers broke Enigma-coded messages with the help of Bombe machines, helping the Allies win their victory.

Code breaking and code making were critical in Allied efforts to undermine the Axis powers. While the Bletchley team enjoyed some victories using the machine that the Germans believed was impenetrable, they were undermined at times by factors such as bureaucracy and gaps in foreign intelligence. For instance, a Bletchley cipher code was broken late in 1941, leading to the sinking of seven merchant ships by the Germans. Delays in catching up with what the Germans knew were in part responsible for the sinking of 1,100 Allied ships and 10,000 deaths in 1942.

Despite the Bletchley team's fervent efforts to crack German code and protect its countrymen and allies, encrypted code shared digitally was practically a brand-new technology. The Bletchley team has passed into legend through Hollywood portrayals and dozens of books, but the Enigma legacy had even more far-reaching effects. By the 1950s, intercepting and cracking code would be a central role in every powerful nation's intelligence efforts. The Enigma introduced a type of warfare that didn't take place in combat, but rather, secretly and behind the scenes. These traits would define the Cold War, a forty-four-year conflict that rose from the ashes of World War II.

PROJECT
A WEB QUEST

Create an internet scavenger hunt to help classmates learn the ins and outs of World War II code breaking. Much like World War II code breakers, clues and guesses will drive peers through the project. Helpful tools for this project include Edcanvas, citbite, WebReel, WordPress, Google Sites, Wikispaces, and Weebly.

- *Make a list of subquestions and hints that relate to a driving question. This list should help plan the website, create scavenger hunt hints and clues, and find the internet-based answers to which visitors should navigate in their scavenger hunt.*

Project-based learning can help you use your computer skills and learn new ways to use technology, such as blogging, podcasts, and web design.

- *The list should contain Internet-based items and assets appropriate for your age group and interesting enough to keep your scavenger hunters engaged.*
- *Include major players in the World War II code-breaking game, such as Alan Turing, and the various codes they cracked, the codes they couldn't crack, and the impact of both those they could and could not figure out in time.*

- Create the website, with an introduction to the driving question and the goal of the scavenger hunt: to thoughtfully and accurately answer the driving question. Based on the list you compiled, create navigational links, subpages, and other website tools to guide your website visitors on their scavenger hunt.
- Create an answer key once all your scavenger hunt pieces are in place. Ask your teacher for guidance on the best time to provide the answer key to your website's visitors. Then, invite peers and the teacher to the website and on the scavenger hunt. Remind them to keep the driving question at the forefront of their research while they work on the project.

CHAPTER FOUR

A WAR OF DILEMMAS

World War II introduced many moral and ethical quandaries revolving around that very question—a question still debated today. As Conrad Crane of the Army Heritage & Education Center expressed the issue in the History Channel's *WWII from Space* documentary, "Will we continue to do what our weapons make possible?"

Many of World War II's most terrifying aspects involved the introduction of sophisticated warplanes, bombers, jets, and submarines. Germany revived one of its World War I weapons, the U-boat, for World War II. These military submarines hunted the Atlantic throughout the entire war. The subs often hunted in what the Germans called wolf packs, keeping the U-boats close together and more effective in hitting targets. Transatlantic shipping vessels carrying goods and other resources, including food, were major U-boat targets. By sinking supply ships, Germany made Britain and other allies vulnerable. World War II U-boats sank about 2,700 ships. When the United States joined the war, its military worked with Britain on U-boat countermeasures that undermined the subs' efficacy.

KAMIKAZE PILOTS

In the Pacific, Allied naval forces were haunted by Japanese *kamikaze* pilots. Kamikaze pilots deliberately killed themselves solely to detonate a bomb or destroy Allied naval vessels or other targets. These pilots wreaked havoc and destruction on Allied naval vessels in the Pacific. Called divine wind or spirit wind by their countrymen, the term *kamikaze* derives from a series of August 1281 typhoons that prevented a Mongolian invasion of Japan.

Allied forces watched, terrified, as Japanese pilots flew directly into military targets, such as destroyers and aircraft carriers. Driven by traditional Japanese values of honor and country before self, these suicide pilots were willing to die for honor and Japan. This self-sacrifice took Allied naval forces by surprise. Even when the Allies shot a kamikaze target, the Japanese pilot would still try to steer his plane toward his target.

In attacks called blitzes, German bombers pounded European cities and nations into submission. German blitzes had no rules; civilian and military targets alike were fair game. German bombers destroyed entire city blocks, killed thousands, decimated or destroyed many of Europe's ancient structures, and forced enemy nations to their knees. Britain was heavily bombed for more than five years, but never capitulated. Its citizens took shelter wherever they could, such as in tube (subway) tunnels. Evidence of Germany's

German bombing, called the Blitz, destroyed many buildings across Britain and parts of cities like London. In this photo, a firefighter pulls a hose through a bombed-out church in London.

World War II bombs in Britain is still visible. For instance, visitors can see pockmarks and holes left in London's nearly one thousand year old Westminster Abbey, a historic and symbolic landmark.

QUESTION: WHY DIDN'T SOMEONE DO SOMETHING?

In a civilized society, a robust system of checks and balances must keep governments in order. But in World War II, the Germans perpetrated the deaths of nearly eight million Jews and other groups they considered undesirable through the Holocaust and other targeted efforts. The Japanese killed millions of Chinese in a campaign that lasted eight years, beginning in the late 1930s and lasting through the end of World War II.

In 1942, shortly after the attack on Pearl Harbor, President Roosevelt ordered the forced relocation of Japanese Americans into internment camps. Between 110,000 and 120,000 people of Japanese ancestry were incarcerated for four years, on American soil, due mostly to fears that they sympathized with America's new enemy and due to an overwhelming American hatred toward the Japanese. For four years, Japanese Americans were forced into their camp communities, shut off from the outside world, and constantly tested to prove their patriotism.

PROJECT
IF YOU COULD GO BACK IN TIME: STOPPING ATROCITIES

The horrors of World War II beg many questions: What did people in Germany and Japan know?

Why did the Italians allow their nation to enter the Axis effort? What did mainstream and other political parties know or do in the Axis nations? Why didn't anyone stop Hitler? Were other Americans unaware that precious American freedoms were denied to Japanese Americans?

- *Research to what extent German, Japanese, and Italian citizens knew about the atrocities carried out in the name of their nationalistic pride. To conduct research, consider tools such as Google Scholar, EndNote, Digital Public Library of America, and SweetSearch.*

- *Consider how state-run media may have obscured facts from the public.*

- *In America, where the First Amendment is held dear, were Americans fully informed of the Japanese internment camps? Were any legal actions taken to help the interned Japanese Americans, or did the government take steps to obscure information not just from the public, but also from the judicial branch of the government?*

- *Where were political opposition groups in the scheme of World War II? Were Hitler and Mussolini unopposed? Did World War II Japan see the rise of any opposition to the imperial order?*

- *Twenty years after World War II, the United States teemed with protestors demanding an end to the Vietnam War. Why was World War II not marked by these same civic protests?*

- *Think about why the public, political opposition groups, or protest groups failed to stop the brutal, deadly, and unfair treatment of ethnic groups around the world during World War II.*

- Following the team's research, form a mock council, committee, political group, opposition

Project-based learning allows for groups to work together and share the responsibilities for research, brainstorming, and developing an end product, like a presentation.

group, or group of concerned citizens in nations like Germany, Japan, Italy, and the United States. To organize the group's efforts and roles, some suggested tools include Stormboard, Google Drive and Hangouts, Livebinders, and Asana. Brainstorm ways the group can solve problems such as:

- Hitler's rise and the deaths carried out at German-run concentration camps
- Japan's and Germany's invasions into neighboring countries and the genocides they carried out
- Mussolini's entry into the Axis powers
- The forced internment of Japanese Americans in the United States
- Make a presentation to the class about your ideas for how to stop World War II's best-known atrocities from occurring. The group's presentation can be a session in which the team acts out its problem-solving, brainstorming, arguments, compromises, conclusions, and solutions.

QUESTION: SHOULD THE ATOMIC BOMB HAVE BEEN DROPPED?

In 1943, Italy surrendered to the Allies, and Italian soldiers began assimilating into the Allied forces to fight the Germans. Between April and May of 1945, the Soviet Red Army stormed across Germany and captured Berlin, waging war for more than two weeks against the paltry German forces left in the Nazi capital. Though the Soviets suffered heavy losses, Hitler, in his underground bunker, knew his grand dreams had been crushed. He committed suicide, and on the night of May 2, General Hasso von Manteuffel and other high-ranking German officials surrendered to the Allies.

Japan kept up the fight, however. While suffering from loss of soldiers, resources, and weaponry, the Japanese code of honor made for a society deeply opposed to surrendering. With millions upon millions dead on both sides of the war, the Allied powers knew the fighting needed to stop—and they knew a powerful weapon would be necessary to bring Japan to surrender.

In a top-secret program called the Manhattan Project, the United States and Canada produced two atomic bombs—the first nuclear weapons ever. On August 6 and 9, 1945, with consent from its major ally, Britain, the United States dropped atomic bombs on the Japanese cities of Hiroshima and Nagasaki. The bombs killed about 130,000 immediately, with its aftereffects (such as radiation and other associated injuries) bringing the number of casualties closer to 300,000.

Japan surrendered on August 15, 1945. The war was over, but in many ways, it had only just begun. While much of the world rejoiced in the war's conclusion, the force and impact of the atomic bombs shocked the world. Nations became obsessed with the threat of nuclear attacks and began to develop nuclear programs to protect themselves. Joseph Stalin, who had been

The second atomic bomb, pictured here mushrooming over Nagasaki, Japan, was dropped on August 9, 1945, and resulted in Japan's ultimate and unconditional surrender—ending World War II.

left out of the Manhattan Project secret and had a tenuous relationship with US president Harry S. Truman, was angered by the deceit. The nuclear race would define the next five decades as the United States and Soviet Union turned on one another during the Cold War.

Nuclear threats continue to plague international relations today, although the atomic bombings of Japan in 1945 remain the first and only use of nuclear weapons. North Korea began carrying out nuclear weapons tests in 2006.

With little intelligence on the closed nation, other world powers do not know the extent of North Korea's nuclear capabilities. Iran has a nuclear program that its leaders claim is for peaceful purposes, but the United States debates this claim often. Atomic bombs brought the deadliest war in history to an end, but the world now lives in the shadow of the threat they introduced.

PROJECT
DEBATING THE A-BOMB

Debate whether the atomic bomb should have been dropped on Hiroshima and Nagasaki, ending the Axis powers' efforts in World War II.

- *Divide the team or class into opposing sides. Have one side develop arguments in favor of dropping the bombs, while the other develops arguments against it. Plan out what your arguments will be before the debate. Some things to consider include:*
  - *Had the bombs not been dropped, would the war have raged on with huge loss of life? Or could another solution have been undertaken?*
  - *The atomic bomb killed many thousands of innocent people, all of them in Japan. Continuing the war would have meant casualties on both sides. How should leaders weigh the lives of enemy civilians*

In project-based learning, students are encouraged to discuss and debate the topics about which they're learning, such as whether the atomic bombs should have been dropped on Japan.

against those of their own soldiers?

- The atomic bomb ushered in a world that lived in the shadow of nuclear war, a state that has continued to exist to this day. Do you think this still would be the case if the atomic bomb had been developed but never used?
- Did the United States and the Allies have no other choice?
- To plan and carry out your debate, consider using tools such as Argunet, bCisive, and Debate Map.

QUESTION: HOW DO RETELLINGS OF WORLD WAR II HELP MODERN AUDIENCES UNDERSTAND THE TRUE IMPACT OF THE WAR?

World War II epitomizes real-life drama: Families separated and massacred in genocides, innocents murdered in retaliatory attacks, widespread destruction, and a legacy of the deadliest kind of weapon ever introduced to the world. It's not surprising that there have been countless attempts to dramatize the war, including novels, TV shows, video games, and movies.

Some World War II operations were highly dramatic in real life, too. For instance, leading up to the Allied invasion of Normandy, the Allied forces snuck in a "ghost army" of inflatable and cardboard tanks and other weaponry. Some machinery was snuck onto the coastline in fake arbors. Just as actors use props, so did the brave fighters of World War II. In doing so, they enabled the Allies to prevail against the Axis.

PROJECT
WALK IN THEIR SHOES

While it's interesting to read or watch other peoples' accounts of World War II, here's your opportunity to make your own. This is your chance to step into the roles of the World War II soldiers who risked everything, and in doing so, changed the course of history.

- *Read a short story or novel about World War II. Then watch a movie that is set during the war.*

Use reputable sources of information to research people who lived through major historical events. Using your research, make those stories your own in your project.

Your school librarian should be able to help you find interesting examples of each.

- *Research several major events in the war. Possibilities include:*
  - *The Battle of Midway*
  - *The Battle of Stalingrad*
  - *The Battle for Britain*
  - *Storming of Normandy*
  - *The Battle of the Bulge*
  - *Operation Barbarossa*

- • *The Battle for Berlin*
- • *The Battle of Shanghai*
- • *The Battle of Iwo Jima*
- • *Operation Torch*
- • *Operation Crusader*
- • *Operation Brevity*
- • *Operation Battleaxe*
- • *The Battle of Gazala*
- • *German-Soviet Invasion of Poland*
- • *The surrender of Paris*
- • *Norwegian Heavy Water Sabotage*
- • **Select one of the events you researched and act it (or highlights from it) out for your class.**
  - • *Write the script out first, and then rehearse it with your cast.*
  - • *Try to depict the parts of the world where the events occurred. Use images to depict the events the team acts out.*
- • **This project should be approached with sensitivity. Team members should refrain from using costumes or iconography that might be controversial or hurtful.**

GLOSSARY

anti-Semitism Hostility toward and prejudice or discrimination against Jewish people.

Aryan A term often used by Nazis or Nazi sympathizers to designate a supposed master race of non-Jewish Caucasians.

atrocity An extremely violent, wrong, and cruel act.

bushidō The Japanese code of the way of the samurai, a code that includes absolute loyalty, martial mastery, and honor until death.

covert Not openly shown or owned by the responsible party.

cryptography Writing, storing, transmitting, and solving secret codes and data.

dictator A political leader who possesses absolute power and wields it in an oppressive or abusive manner.

expansionism A policy of territorial or economic expansion.

genocide The deliberate and systemic massacre or extermination of a national, racial, political, or cultural group.

internment Prison confinement, especially for political or military purposes.

isolationism The policy of isolating one's country from the affairs of other nations.

nationalist Referring to a sense of loyalty and devotion to a nation, often characterized by a sense of superiority over other nations.

occupation The control of an area by a foreign military force.

propaganda Ideas, facts, allegations, and rumors spread to deliberately further a cause and damage an opposing cause.

war crimes Serious violations of the law of war, marked by individual criminal responsibility.

FOR MORE INFORMATION

Canadian Centre for the Victims
    of Torture (CCVT)
194 Jarvis Street, 2nd Floor
Toronto, ON M5B 2B7
Canada
(416) 363-1066
Website: http://ccvt.org
Part of the Canadian Centre for
    the Investigation and Preven-
    tion of Torture, the CCVT
    provides specialized coun-
    seling, legal aid, and care for
    survivors, and aids in efforts
    to end torture and war.

The Center for Holocaust and
    Genocide Studies (CHGS)
University of Minnesota
214 Social Sciences Building
267 19th Avenue S
Minneapolis, MN 55455
(612) 624-9007
Website: https://cla.umn.edu
    /chgs
Facebook and YouTube:
    @chgsumn
This center is dedicated to ana-
    lyzing and understanding the
    causes, impacts, and legacies
    of the Holocaust, other geno-
    cides, and mass violence.

Facing History and Ourselves
16 Hurd Road
Brookline, MA 02445
(617) 232-1595
Contact: https://www
    .facinghistory.org/contact
Facebook & Twitter:
    @facinghistory
This nonprofit organization
    engages students of diverse
    backgrounds in an exam-
    ination of racism, prejudice,
    and anti-Semitism to pro-
    mote the development of
    a more humane and in-
    formed citizenry.

Library and Archives Canada
395 Wellington Street
Ottawa, ON K1A 0N4
Canada
(866) 578-7777
Facebook and Twitter:
    @libraryarchives
World War II was the third ma-
    jor conflict in which Can-
    ada participated, costing
    forty-five thousand Canadi-
    an lives. These archives offer
    research, virtual exhibitions,
    open records, and databases.

Library of Congress
101 Independence Avenue, SE
Washington, DC 20540
(202) 707-5000
Website: https://www.loc.gov/rr
/program/bib/WW2
/WW2bib.html
Facebook and Twitter:
@libraryofcongress
The Library of Congress has
extensive war archives.
Interviews, photos, map
collections, exhibitions,
and oral histories only
scratch the surface of this
extensive collection.

Nanking Massacre Project
Yale University Divinity Library
409 Prospect Street
New Haven, CT 06511
(203) 432-5290
Website: http://web.library.yale
.edu/divinity/nanking
This Project maintains a digital
archive of documents and
photographs from the American missionaries who witnessed the rape and massacre
at Nanjing.

National Archives
8601 Adelphi Road
College Park, MD 20740
(866) 272-6272
Facebook: @usnationalarchives
Twitter: @USNatArchives
YouTube:
@USNationalArchives
The National Archives gives visitors direct access to World
War II resources, including
military records, archives
that survived the war,
speeches, information on
covert codes, photos, and
war criminals' records.

United States Holocaust
Memorial Museum
(USHMM)
100 Raoul Wallenberg Place, SW
Washington, DC 20024
(202) 488-0400
Website:
https://www.ushmm.org
Facebook: @holocaustmuseum
Twitter: @HolocaustMuseum
The USHMM collects Holo-
caust materials, such as pri-
mary sources, in a diverse
offering of formats.

FOR FURTHER READING

Bains, Alisha, ed., *World War II: A Political and Diplomatic History of the Modern World*. New York, NY: Britannica Educational Publishing, 2017.

Bartrop, Paul R. *A Biographical Encyclopedia of Contemporary Genocide: Portraits of Evil and Good*. Santa Barbara, CA: ABC-CLIO, 2012.

Burgan, Michael. *Japanese American Internment* (Eyewitness to World War II). North Mankato, MN: Compass Point Books, 2018.

Darman, Peter. *Attack on Pearl Harbor: America Enters World War II*. New York, NY: Rosen Publishing, 2013.

Darman, Peter. *The Battle of the Atlantic: Naval Warfare from 1939–1945*. New York, NY: Rosen Publishing, 2012.

Darman, Peter. *The Holocaust and Life Under Nazi Occupation*. New York, NY: Rosen Publishing 2013.

Ellis, Catherine, ed., *Key Figures of World War II: Biographies of War*. New York, NY: Britannica Educational Publishing, 2016.

Mann, Tara, ed., *World War I: A Political and Diplomatic History of the Modern World*. New York, NY: Britannica Educational Publishing, 2017.

Servin, Morgan. *World War II Close Up: The War Chronicles*. New York, NY: Rosen Publishing, 2016.

Throp, Claire. *The Horrors of the Holocaust* (Deadly History). North Mankato, MN: Capstone, 2018.

Timmons, Angie. *The Nanjing Massacre*. New York, NY: Rosen Publishing, 2018.

BIBLIOGRAPHY

Beasley, W.G. *Japanese Imperialism 1894–1945*. Oxford, UK: Oxford University Press, 1987 (reprint 1999).

Chang, Iris. *The Rape of Nanking: The Forgotten Holocaust of World War II*. New York, NY: BasicBooks, 1997 (reprint 2014).

Del Pilar Álvarez, María, et al. "The Limits of Forgiveness in International Relations: Groups Supporting the Yasukuni Shrine in Japan and Political Tensions in East Asia." Janus.Net: E-Journal of International Relations, vol. 7, no. 2, Nov2016–Apr2017, pp. 26–49. EBSCOhost, search.ebscohost.com/login.aspx?direct=true&db=a9h&AN=120427040&site=ehost-live.

History Channel. *WWII from Space*. History Channel, 2015. https://www.youtube.com/watch?v=TdBSwhms7O4.

Levinson, David. "Xenophobia." World History: The Modern Era, ABC-CLIO, 2017. http://worldhistory.abc-clio.com/Search/Display/421575.

Magelssen, Brian N. "The Willful Ignorance of Japan's Past." Chinese American Forum, vol. 31, no. 1, Jul–Sep2015, pp. 15–20. http://caforumonline.net/CAFHandlerPDF.ashx?ID=416.

National Geographic. "Inside WWII. National Geographic/YouTube, 2016. https://www.youtube.com/watch?v=uze8P5tPOqk. Retrieved September 26, 2017.

"Nationalism." World History: The Modern Era, ABC-CLIO, 2017, worldhistory.abc-clio.com/Search/Display/309385.

Neier, Aryeh. *War Crimes: Brutality, Genocide, Terror, and the Struggle for Justice*. New York, NY: Times Books (Random House), 1998.

"Sino-Japanese War of 1937–1945." World History: The Modern Era, ABC-CLIO, 2017, worldhistory.abc-clio.com/Search/Display/309967.

INDEX

ABOUT THE AUTHOR

Angie Timmons is a writer who studied journalism and sociology at Texas Tech University. She has worked in print news and technical and proposal writing. She has written four other titles for Rosen: *The Nanjing Massacre, Everything You Need to Know About Racism, Real-World Projects to Explore the Cold War,* and *How to Create Digital Portfolios to Show What You Know.* She lives in a Dallas suburb with her husband, Jason, and their three cats.

PHOTO CREDITS

Cover, p. 1 Phovoir/Shutterstock.com; p. 3 Ollyy/Shutterstock.com; p. 4 Pressmaster/Shutterstock.com; p. 5 Bettmann/Getty Images; p. 8 Hulton Archive/Archive Photos/Getty Images; p. 11 Universal History Archive/Universal Images Group/Getty Images; p. 14 Underwood Archives/Archive Photos/Getty Images; p. 18 Wavebreakmedia/iStock/Thinkstock; p. 22 National Archives; p. 25 Jeffrey Greenberg/Universal Images Group/Getty Images; p. 27 ullstein bild/Getty Images; p. 32 Andrew Burton/Getty Images; p. 35 The Washington Post/Getty Images; p. 37 Glyn Kirk/AFP/Getty Images; p. 39 Bletchley Park Trust/SSPL/Getty Images; p. 41 SeventyFour/Shutterstock.com; p. 45 Central Press/Hulton Archive/Getty Images; p. 48 Jupiterimages/PHOTOS.com/Thinkstock; p. 51 Library of Congress, Prints and Photographs Division; p. 53 Monkey Business Images/Shutterstock.com; p. 55 © iStockphoto.com/mediaphotos.

Design: Nelson Sá; Layout: Raúl Rodriguez; Editor: Amelie von Zumbusch; Photo Researcher: Nicole DiMella